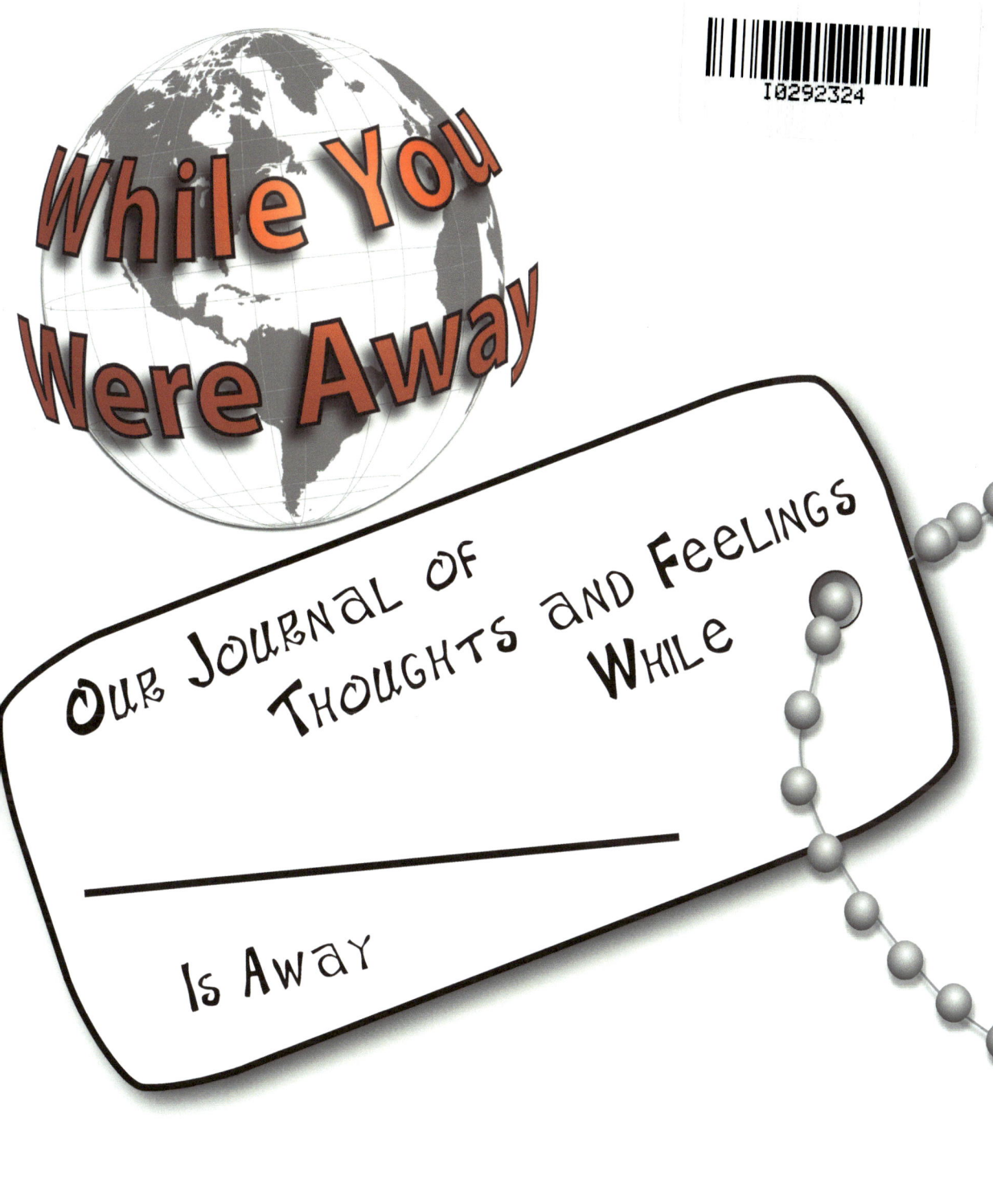

While You Were Away

Our Journal of Thoughts and Feelings While _____ Is Away

By: _____

_____

Written At: _____

Date: _____

WATCH TV

Ride a Bike

Go for a Hike

Go Swimming

ROLLERBLADING

Walk in th

Dinner Out

Try a New Activity

Go for a Driv

Go to a Movie

Watch a Video

WALK IN THE SUNSHINE

Bird Watching

Snow Boa

Fly a Kite

Bar-B-Que Tonigh

Skiing

Go Swimming

COOK DINNER TOGETH

Wash the Dishes Together

Have a Picnic

Go Shopping

Play a Board Game

DEPLOYMENT INFO

Deployment Address:
_____
_____
_____
_____
_____

Things I Could Write About:
_____
_____
_____
_____
_____
_____
_____

Millitary Contacts:
_____
_____

Deployment Email Address:

Military Familly Support:
_____
_____
_____

EMERGENCY contacts:
_____
_____
_____
_____

Other:
_____
_____

Our Weekly Routine

Family Member	Activity
Sunday	
Monday	
Tuesday	
Wednesday	
Thursday	
Friday	
Saturday	

Family

Fearful

Hurt

Rejected

peaceful

challenged

RESTED

Panicked

TERRIBLE

Love

Beautiful

Vulnerable

Exhausted

Mad

OUTRAGED

carious

Miser

Fun Things To Do, While You Are Away

#'s to Know

Doctor:

Dentist:

Insurance Rep:

Financial Planner:

Bank:

Public Service Unit:

Walk-in Clinic:

Hospital:

Children's Hospital:

Poison Control:

Neighbour:

Emergency: 911

Daycare:

Emergency Daycare:

Mechanic:

Landlord / Base Housing:

Plumber:

Electrician:

Kennel:

Plumber:

Inspired

nutty

Worried

Wonderful

Shocked

Uneasy

Sad

Talkative

Silly

overwhelmed

Tense

Relaxed

Abandoned

Scared

Relieved

Troubled

lonely

Unsettled

Ignored

Isolated

PANICKED

Cheerful

Rejected

Empty

Annoyed

Our Worries

Our Fears

Fearful

Hurt

Rejected

Peaceful

Challenged

RESTED

Panicked

TERRIBLE

Love

Beautiful

Vulnerable

Exhausted

Mad

OUTRAGED

Precarious

Miserable

Five things we'll do to keep healthy.

Watch TV
Ride a Bike
Go for a Hike
Go Swimming
Rollerblading
Walk in the Mal
Dinner Out
Try a New Activity
Go for a Drive
Go to a Movie
Walk in the Sunshine
Watch a Video
Snow Boarding
Bird Watching
Fly a Kite
Bar-B-Que Tonight
Skiing
Go Swimming
Cook Dinner Together
Wash the Dishes Together
Have a Picnic
Go Shopping
Play a Board Game
Try a New Recipe Together

I Dreamt Last Night That...

Family Policing Report

Issued On: _____   Filed By: _____

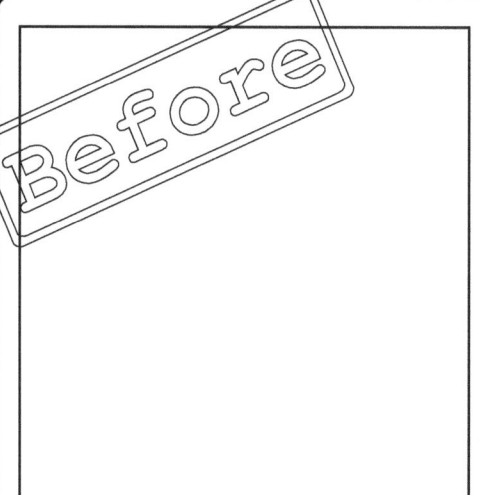

Mug Shot Date: _____   Mug Shot Date: _____

Issued Against: _____

Problem: _____

Solution: _____

Outcome: _____

WATCH TV
Ride a Bike
Go for a Hike
Go Swimming
ROLLERBLADING
Walk in the Ma
Dinner Out
Try a New Activity
Go for a Drive
Go to a Movie
Watch a Video
WATCH THE SUNSET
Bird Watching
Snow Boarding
Fly a Kite
Bar-B-Que Tonight
Skiing
Go Swimming
COOK DINNER TOGETHER
Wash the Dishes Together
Have a Picnic
Go Shopping
Play a Board Game

Try a New Recipe Together

Where in the World?

Country:

City or Town:

Province, State or County:

Average Temperature in Summer:

Average Temperature in Winter:

Temperature at Night:

Sun Rise:

Sun Set:

Time Difference:

Language Spoken:

Currency:

Capital City:

Travel Time:

Travel Distance:

Build an Indoor Tent · Go to the Library · HAVE A PARTY · Go to a Museum · WATCH A SUNSET · Mini Golf · Play Charades · Camp in the Backyard · Gardening · Star Gazing · Watch a Sunrise · Take Photographs · Press Leaves or Flowers · GO TO A BOOKSTORE · Bake a Cake · Play Frisbee · Try Rollerblading · Go Bowling · Do Crafts · Go to the Art Gallery

While you are away, we'll be...

Our Adventures

Time Change

12:00

Our Time | +/- | Their Time

When we are...

- Waking up
- Getting dressed
- Eating breakfast
- At school / work
- Eating lunch
- Having dinner
- Watching TV
- Going to bed
- Sleeping

Inspired

Nutty

Worried

Wonderful

Shocked

Uneasy

Sad

Talkative

Silly

overwhelmed

Tense

Relaxed

Abandoned

Scared

Relieved

Troubled

lonely

Unsettled

Ignored

Isolated

PANICKED

Cheerful

Rejected

Empty

Annoyed

DESPAIRING

I'm so tired...
_____
_____
_____
_____
_____
_____
_____
_____

I was surprised to hear from you today...
_____
_____
_____
_____
_____
_____
_____
_____

Watch TV

Ride a Bike

Go for a Hike

Go Swimming

Rollerblading

Walk in the Mal

Dinner Out

Try a New Activity

Go for a Drive

Go to a Movie

Watch a Video

Walk in the Sunshine

Bird Watching

Snow Boarding

Fly a Kite

Bar-B-Que Tonight

Skiing

Go Swimming

Cook Dinner Together

Wash the Dishes Together

Have a Picnic

Go Shopping

Play a Board Game

Try a New Recipe Together

Family Policing Report

Issued On: _____ Filed By: _____

Mug Shot Date: _____   Mug Shot Date: _____

Issued Against: _____

Problem: _____

Solution: _____

Outcome: _____

Write a list of all the good and bad things that have come out of having someone in your life away.

The Pros
The Good Things

_____
_____
_____
_____
_____
_____
_____
_____
_____
_____
_____
_____
_____
_____
_____
_____
_____
_____
_____
_____

The Cons
The Tough Things

_____
_____
_____
_____
_____
_____
_____
_____
_____
_____
_____
_____
_____
_____
_____
_____
_____
_____
_____
_____

Friends
The Family We Choose

I'm So Lonely...

If you were here right now we'd...

Where we went: _____
_____
What we did: _____
_____
_____
Worst thing: _____
_____
Best thing: _____
_____
Date: _____

Fearful

Hurt

Rejected

peaceful

challenged

RESTED

Panicked

TERRIBLE

Love

Beautiful

Vulnerable

Exhausted

Mad

OUTRAGED

Precarious

Miserable

It was so good to hear your voice...

Watch TV
Ride a Bike
Go for a Hike
Go Swimming
Rollerblading
Walk in the Ma
Dinner Out
Try a New Activity
Go for a Drive
Go to a Movie
Watch a Video
Walk in the Sunshine
Snow Boardin
Bird Watching
Fly a Kite
Bar-B-Que Tonight
Skiing
Go Swimming
COOK DINNER TOGETHE
Wash the Dishes Together
Have a Picnic
Go Shopping
Play a Board Game
Try a New Recipe Together

FINISH THE DESIGN

By:

Inspired

nutty

Worried

Wonderful

Shocked

Unrasy

Sad

Talkative

Silly

overwhelmed

Tense

Relaxed

Abandoned

Scared

Relieved

Troubled

lonely

Unsettled

Ignored

Isolated

PANICKED

Cheerful

Rejected

Empty

Annoyed

DESPAIRING

Family Deployment Medals

Awarded To:
_____

Awarded To:
_____

In Recognition of:
_____
_____
_____
_____
_____
_____

In Recognition of:
_____
_____
_____
_____
_____
_____

Family Deployment Medal

Awarded To:
_____

In Recognition of:
_____
_____
_____
_____
_____
_____
_____
_____
_____
_____
_____
_____
_____
_____
_____
_____
_____
_____
_____

WATCH TV
Ride a Bike
Go for a Hike
Go Swimming
ROLLERBLADING
Walk in the Mal
Dinner Out
Try a New Activity
Go for a Drive
Go to a Movie
Watch a Video
WALK IN THE SUNSHINE
Bird Watching
Snow Boarding
Fly a Kite
Bar-B-Que Tonight
Skiing
Go Swimming
COOK DINNER TOGETHER
Wash the Dishes Together
Have a Picnic
Go Shopping
Play a Board Game
Try a New Recipe Together

I'm feeling strong today...
_____
_____
_____
_____
_____
_____
_____
_____

I'm not sure how much longer I can do this...
_____
_____
_____
_____
_____
_____
_____
_____

Our Adventures

Family Deployment Medals

Awarded To:
_____

Awarded To:
_____

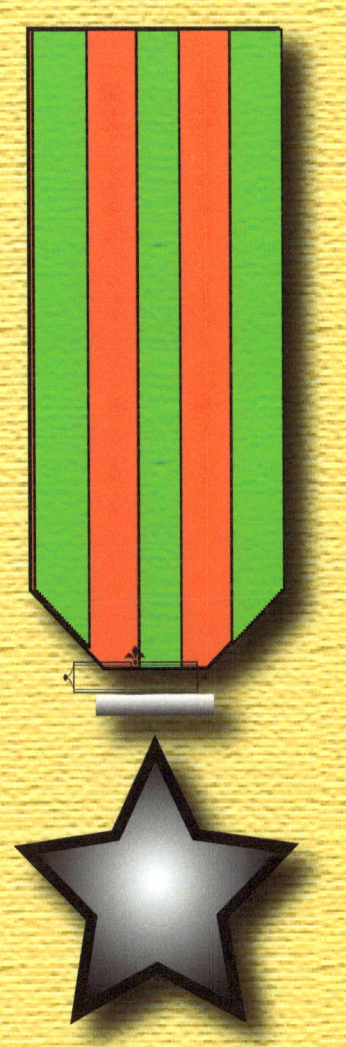
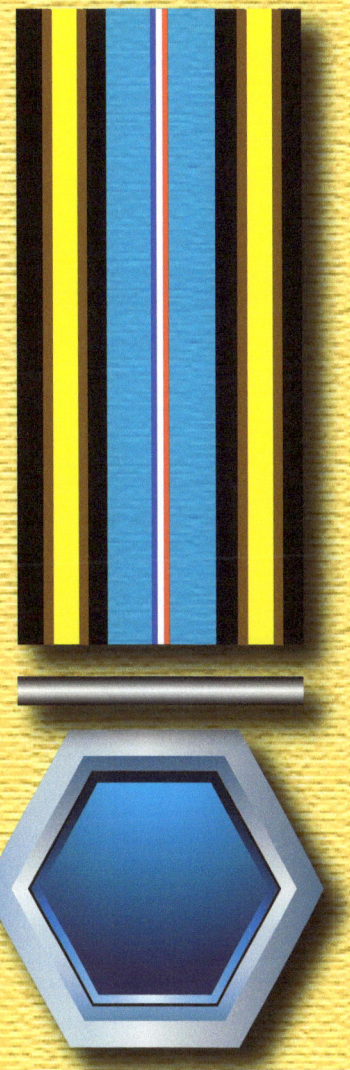

In Recognition of:
_____
_____
_____
_____
_____
_____
_____

In Recognition of:
_____
_____
_____
_____
_____
_____
_____

I support you but it's really hard…

Support our troops

Fearful

Hurt

Rejected

peaceful

challenged

RESTED

Panicked

TERRIBLE

Love

Beautiful

Vulnerable

Exhausted

Mad

OUTRAGED

Precarious

Miserabl

I'm So Excited...

Deployment Certificate

Family Seal of Approval

Awarded To:

In Recognition of:

Deployment Coupons

Save Save Save Save Save Save Save Save Save Save Save Save

Family Coupon — Not redeemable with any other offer. Valid only durring Deployment. Recieve one collect and take out garbage. WoW!!

Family Coupon — Not redeemable with any other offer. Valid only durring Deployment. Recieve one car wash. WoW!!

Family Coupon — Not redeemable with any other offer. Valid only durring Deployment. Recieve one night of no complaining! WoW!!

Family Coupon — Not redeemable with any other offer. Valid only durring Deployment. Recieve one movie night together. WoW!!

Family Coupon — Not redeemable with any other offer. Valid only durring Deployment. Recieve one wash and dry of dishes. WoW!!

Family Coupon — Not redeemable with any other offer. Valid only durring Deployment. Recieve one meal prepared and served. WoW!!

Family Coupon — Not redeemable with any other offer. Valid only durring Deployment. Recieve one bedroom cleaning. WoW!!

Family Coupon — Not redeemable with any other offer. Valid only durring Deployment. Recieve one trip to fast food of your choice. WoW!!

Family Coupon — Not redeemable with any other offer. Valid only durring Deployment. Recieve one night of homework help. WoW!!

Family Coupon — Not redeemable with any other offer. Valid only durring Deployment. Recieve one house vacumed. WoW!!

Save Save Save Save Save Save Save Save Save Save Save Save

WATCH TV

Ride a Bike

Go for a Hike

Go Swimming

ROLLERBLADING

Walk in the Mall

Dinner Out

Try a New Activity

Go for a Drive

Go to a Movie

Watch a Video

WALK IN THE SUNSHINE

Bird Watching

Snow Boarding

Fly a Kite

Bar-B-Que Tonight

Skiing

Go Swimming

COOK DINNER TOGETHER

Wash the Dishes Together

Have a Picnic

Go Shopping

Play a Board Game

Try a New Recipe Together

Life without you
isn't the same...
_____
_____
_____
_____
_____
_____
_____

There is so much work
to do! I wish you were here to...
_____
_____
_____
_____
_____
_____
_____
_____

I Dreamt Last Night That...

WATCH TV

Ride a Bike

Go for a Hike

Go Swimming

ROLLERBLADING

Walk in the Ma

Dinner Out

Try a New Activity

Go for a Drive

Go to a Movie

Watch a Video

WALK IN THE SUNSHINE

Bird Watching

Snow Boardin

Fly a Kite

Bar-B-Que Tonight

Skiing

Go Swimming

COOK DINNER TOGETHE

Wash the Dishes Together

Have a Picnic

Go Shopping

Play a Board Game

Try a New Recipe Together

I'm feeling stronger today...

Some days we feel like you've been away for a life time...

Inspired

Nutty

Worried

Wonderful

Shocked

Uneasy

Sad

Talkative

Silly

overwhelmed

Tense

Relaxed

Abandoned

Scared

Relieved

Troubled

lonely

Ignored

Unsettled

Isolated

PANICKED

Cheerful

Rejected

Empty

Annoyed

DESPAIRING

FINISH THE DESIGN

By:

Us Before

_____
_____
_____
_____
_____
_____
_____
_____
_____
_____
_____
_____
_____
_____
_____
_____
_____
_____

Us After

_____
_____
_____
_____
_____
_____
_____
_____
_____
_____
_____
_____
_____
_____
_____
_____
_____
_____

How We've Changed

I wish I knew what you were doing right now...

Inspired
Worried
nutty
Wonderful
Shocked
Uneasy
Sad
Talkative
Silly
overwhelmed
Tense
Relaxed
Abandoned
Scared
Relieved
Troubled
lonely
Ignored
Unsettled
Isolated
PANICKED
Cheerful
Rejected
Empty
Annoyed
DESPAIRING

All the things we love about you

Fearful

Hurt

Rejected

peaceful

Challenged

RESTED

Panicked

TERRIBLE

Love

Beautiful

Vulnerable

Exhausted

Mad

OUTRAGED

Precarious

Miserabl

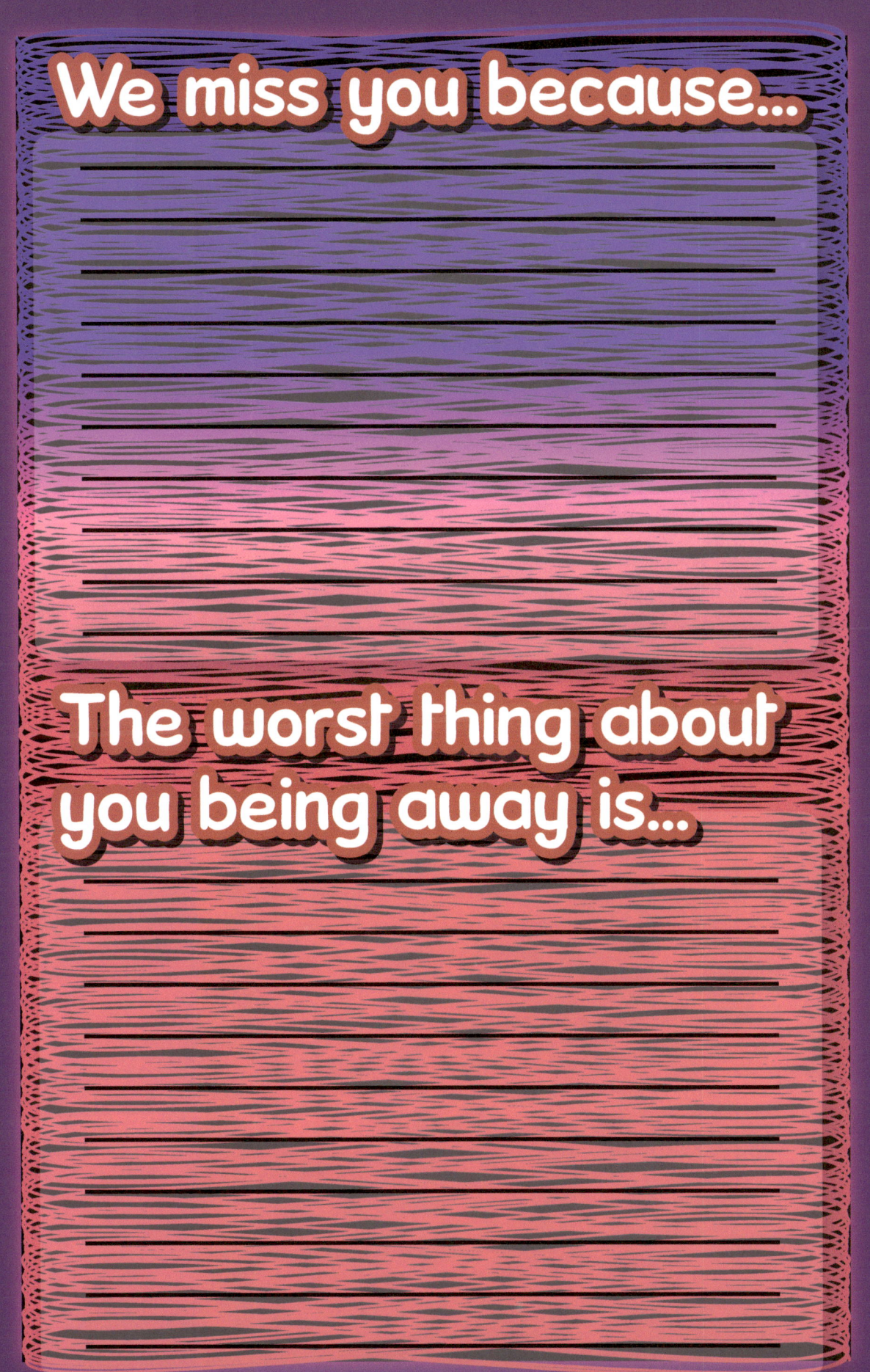

We wanted to pick up the phone and call you today..

Watch TV
Ride a Bike
Go for a Hike
Go Swimming
Rollerblading
Walk in the Mal
Dinner Out
Try a New Activity
Go for a Drive
Go to a Movie
Watch a Video
Bird Watching
Snow Boarding
Fly a Kite
Bar-B-Que Tonight
Skiing
Go Swimming
Cook Dinner Together
Wash the Dishes Together
Have a Picnic
Go Shopping
Play a Board Game
Try a New Recipe Together

SCHOOL UPDATES

We really missed you not being here today...

_____
_____
_____
_____
_____
_____
_____
_____
_____
_____
_____
_____

When are you coming back?

Inspired nutty

Worried Wonderful

Shocked Uneasy

Sad

Talkative

Silly

Overwhelmed

Tense

Relaxed

Abandoned

Scared Relieved

Troubled

lonely

Unsettled

Ignored

Isolated

PANICKED

Cheerful

Rejected

Empty

Annoyed

DESPAIRING

FINISH THE DESIGN

WATCH TV
Ride a Bike
Go for a Hike
Go Swimming
ROLLERBLADING
Walk in the Mal
Dinner Out
Try a New Activity
Go for a Drive
Go to a Movie
Watch a Video
WALK IN THE SUNSHINE
Snow Boarding
Bird Watching
Fly a Kite
Bar-B-Que Tonight
Skiing
Go Swimming
COOK DINNER TOGETHER
Wash the Dishes Together
Have a Picnic
Go Shopping
Play a Board Game

Try a New Recipe Together

When You Get Back We Will...

When You Get Back...

When You Get Back...

© Megan Egerton and John Willman 2010 All rights reserved. No part of this book may be reproduced in any form without the written permission from the authors.

For more information contact:
www.whileyouwereaway.org

Notes:

www.ingramcontent.com/pod-product-compliance
Lightning Source LLC
Chambersburg PA
CBHW041522220426
43669CB00002B/25